Contents

Knooking workshop

Casting on

  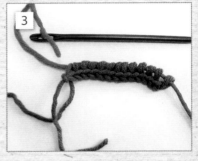

Start by casting on chain stitches: draw a length of yarn in a contrasting colour through the eye on the end of the hook (length twice the width of the item + 20cm/7¾in). Knot to secure, if required. Cast on the required number of chain stitches. The stitches are now worked onto these chains.

Hold the hook with the chain stitches upside down. The loop on the hook is the first stitch. Insert the hook in the horizontal thread on the back of the second chain, draw the yarn through and leave the loop on the hook as a stitch. Keep repeating this sequence.

At the end of the row, pull the yarn to the left through the stitches until all the stitches are on the cord. Then turn the work around.

First row = wrong side

 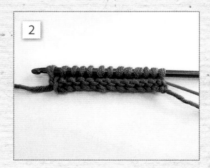 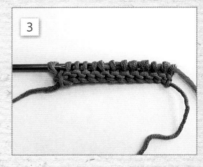

Insert the hook in the first stitch from right to left, draw yarn through, and leave the loop on the hook as a stitch. Keep repeating this sequence to achieve plain stitches.

At the end of the row, pull the cord (to the right) out of the stitches of the previous row.

Then draw the yarn (to the left) through the stitches you just made until all the stitches are back on the cord.

Veronika Hug

Knooking

19 projects to knit with a crochet hook

Introduction

It's time to get acquainted with "knooking".
You'll be amazed to see that although the results look knitted, they are actually created using a type of crochet hook. The name comes from the combination of the word "hook" and "knitting" because, effectively, you are crocheting your knitting. So, if you're a fan of all things knitted or crocheted, chances are you'll also love knooking.

At first, I was a sceptic, but then I got to grips with the knooking hook – which has a crochet hook at the front and an eye at the end for threading the yarn. I was so convinced by the results that I thought I'd write an entire book about this fantastic hybrid craft.

I have tried everything that you could possibly knook and, trust me, you really can do anything. However, I do recommend starting with something easy (in the same way you would when learning to knit or crochet). My advice is to start by choosing a design that is worked in rows – that's knooking at its easiest. Once you're comfortable with using the hook and yarn, you'll soon be able to advance to some of the more challenging designs.

To make it simple, the projects are graded by how easy they are:

Levels of difficulty
      ✶ = quick and easy
    ✶✶ = requires a little practice
  ✶✶✶ = advanced

Note

On pages 4 to 9, you will find information on the knooking techniques used in this book as well as the basic crochet stitches and some helpful finishing off techniques.

I hope you enjoy this new technique as much as I do. I would be delighted if, one day, knooking features just as much in the craft world as knitting and crocheting.

Happy knooking!

Veronika Hug

Plain (or knit) stitch

Insert the hook in the stitch from right to left, draw yarn through and leave the loop on the hook as a stitch.

Garter stitch

Knook plain (or knit) stitches in both rows, i.e. right and wrong sides.

Stocking stitch

Knook plain stitches on the right side, and purl stitches on the wrong side. The stitches on the front of the item are straight.

Stocking stitch, twisted

Knook plain stitches on the right side, and twisted purl stitches on the wrong side. On the front of the item, the stitches of every second row are twisted.

Purl stitch

1

Place the yarn in front of the work. Insert the hook into the stitch from left to right, lightly pulling the stitch to the right with the hook, and then insert from behind.

2

Pull the yarn through. This stitch requires a little practice. It is used to create the stocking or reverse stocking stitch effect. The stitches on the front of the item are straight.

Knooking workshop

Purl stitches, twisted

Place the yarn in front of the work. Insert the hook into the stitch from right to left, draw the yarn through and pull to the back. The stitches on the front of the item are twisted.

Increasing

Knook the stitch plain, then insert the hook in the loop below the stitch you have just made.

Pull the yarn through. The loop remains on the hook as an increased stitch.

Decreasing

Decreasing stitches together: insert the hook in the next two stitches, working from right to left.

Draw the yarn through both loops on the hook.

Casting off/crocheting off

Insert the hook in the stitch from right to left, draw the yarn through and pull through both loops on the hook. Repeat this sequence until all stitches have been cast off. Pull the cord out at the end.

Knooking in rounds

Casting on

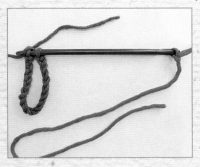

Draw the cord through the stitches until all the stitches are on the cord. Take up the second half of the stitches, and leave on the hook.

First round

1

The loop on the hook is the first stitch. Insert the hook in the diagonal thread on the back of the chain, draw the yarn through, and leave the loop on the hook as the first stitch. Repeat until you have completed half the work.

2

Draw the cord through the stitches until all the stitches are on the cord. Take up the stitches from the second half of the chain, and likewise leave them on the hook.

Stocking stitch in rounds

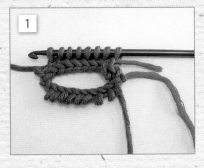

1

Insert the hook in the first stitch from right to left and draw the yarn through. Knook the following stitches in the same way until you have about half the stitches on the hook.

2

Draw the cord through the stitches until the end is still two to three stitches from the knooked stitches.

3

Continue knooking about half the stitches, and keep drawing the cord through to just before the knooked stitches.

Basic crochet and finishes

Chain stitch

Place the yarn from back to front around the hook and draw through the stitch.

Slip stitch

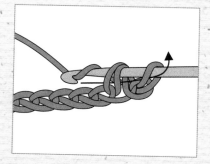

Insert the hook in the stitch, yarn around hook, and draw through the loop on the hook.

Single crochet (UK double)

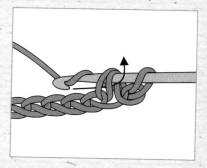

Insert the hook in the stitch, yarn around hook and draw through one loop. Draw the yarn through both loops on the hook.

Half double (UK half treble)

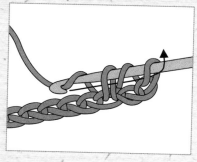

Yarn around hook and insert in stitch. Draw the yarn through the stitch. Draw the yarn through again and pull through all three loops on the hook.

Double (UK treble)

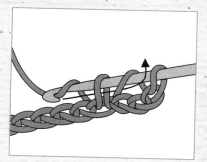

Yarn around hook, insert in stitch and draw yarn through. Yarn around hook and draw through the first two loops, yarn around hook again and draw through the two remaining loops.

Decreasing stitches together

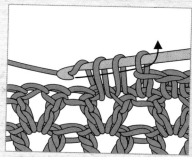

Single crochet (UK double): insert the hook in the stitch and draw the yarn through. Insert the hook in the next stitch and again draw the yarn through. Draw the yarn through again through all three loops.

Several stitches in one stitch

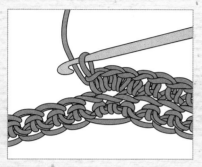

To increase stitches, work the required number of stitches into the same stitch.

Kitchener stitch

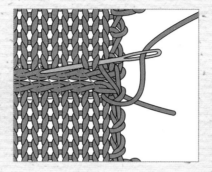

Place items together with the front facing up. Take up one stitch of the top piece with the hook and draw the yarn through. Take up the same stitch on the other piece and draw the yarn through.

Saddle stitch

Insert the hook from back to front through both pieces, work one stitch back to the right (backstitch), move hook to the left on the wrong side and push through in front of the last exit point. Work the back stitch of the following stitches into the previous exit point. With the following stitches, insert the needle in the back stitch of the previous exit point.

Weaving fringes

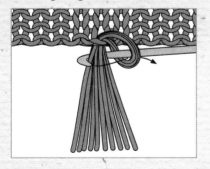

Cut yarn to length (length of fringe x 2 + 1cm/⅜in for the knot). Insert the crochet hook through a stitch, catch threads in the middle and draw through in a loop. Take the threads from right to left and draw through the loop. Tie a knot.

Pompom

Cut two cardboard circles of the desired diameter. Cut a hole in the middle and place the two circles together. Thread the yarn on a wool needle and feed through the middle, and wind loosely, but densely around the ring.

Cut through the threads around the outer edge, and pry the rings slightly apart. Tie a double length of yarn tightly between the cardboard rings and knot securely. Carefully remove the cardboard.

Outdoors

Some new favourites for when you're out and about! There's a range of trendy knooking designs for the whole family.

Striped hat

Triangle neck wrap

Children's striped beanie

Colourful looped scarf

Wrist warmers

Men's scarf

Stylish bag

Green beanie

Marled hat

Size: 52–56cm (20½-22in)   •   Level of difficulty: ✳

Materials

- Wool acrylic blend –, yardage approximately 100m (328ft) /100g (3½oz): 200g (7oz) red marl
- Knooking hook 10/J (6mm)

Garter stitch: plain (or knit) stitches in both directions

Tension: 12 stitches and 20 rows = 10 x 10cm (4 x 4in)

How to do it

Chain 30 stitches, transfer to the knooking hook and work 50cm (19¾in) in garter stitch. Then crochet off the stitches.

Finishing off

Sew up the hat seam using kitchener stitch and pull up the straight edge. Take up every second edge stitch with yarn and pull tight. Make a pompon of about 8cm (3¼in) diameter and sew to the middle of the hat.

The perfect fit

This day ...

... belongs to us!

Striped hat

Size: 52–56cm (20½-22in) • Level of difficulty: ✱

Materials

- Wool acrylic blend – yardage approximately 100m (328ft)/100g (3½oz): 100g (3½oz) each in white, pink and burgundy
- Knooking hook 10/J (6mm)

Garter stitch: plain (or knit) stitches in both directions

Stipe sequence: * 4 rows each in white, pink, burgundy, pink, repeat from *

Tension: 12 stitches and 24 rows = 10 x 10cm (4 x 4in)

How to do it

Chain 24 stitches in white, then transfer to the knooking hook and work 50cm (19¾in) in garter stitch. Then cast off (ideally after 4 rows in pink).

Finishing up

Sew up the hat seam using kitchener stitch and pull up the straight edge where you changed colours. Take up every second edge stitch with yarn and pull tight. Make a pompom of about 8cm (3¼in) diameter in all three colours, and sew to the middle of the hat.

Colourful looped scarf

Size: 15 x 120cm (6 x 47¼in) (circumference) • Level of difficulty: ✴

Materials
- Wool acrylic blend – yardage approximately 165m (541ft)/100g (3½oz): 200g (7oz) multi-coloured yarn
- Knooking hook 10/J (6mm)

Ribbing: Cast on a multiple of 4 + 2 + 2 edge stitches. Right side: edge stitch, knit 2 plain, knit 2 purl alternating, ending with knit 2 and 1 edge stitch. Wrong stitch: knook stitches as they appear. Tension ribbing: 16 stitches and 23 rows = 10 x 10cm (4 x 4in) (very slightly stretched).

How to do it
Chain 24 stitches, then transfer to knooking hook and work 120cm (47¼in) in rib stitch. Cast off.

Finishing off
Turn the scarf by 180 degrees and sew up the casting on and off edges in kitchener stitch.

Rainbow colours ...

... to brighten your day

Triangle neck wrap

Size: 170 x 60cm (67 x 23½in) (without fringes) • Level of difficulty: ✱✱

Materials

- Alpaca wool nylon blend – yardage approximately 65m (213ft 3in) /50g (1¾oz): 300g (10½oz) pink
- Knooking hook 10/J (6mm)

Stocking stitch: right side plain (or knit), wrong side purl

How to do it

Work as indicated in the diagram. Start with the stitches before the pattern (MS), then repeat the pattern and finish with the stitches after the pattern. Only the rows on the right sides are shown.

Purl all the stitches and yarn around hook on the wrong side. Work rows 1–38 once, then keep repeating rows 33–38 and increase appropriately until the garment is of the desired width (our version measures 60cm/23½in). Then continue repeating rows 39–44 until only 18 stitches are left. Finish with rows 45–74 and cast off the last 3 stitches.

Finishing off

Using a double thread, work fringes approximately 14cm (5½in) long into each yarn around hook along the angled sides of the wrap. The wrap can be worn on either side.

Diagram

(Chart rows, right-side rows numbered 1–73 odd, symbols as below)

Row	
73	+ ↓ +
71	+ U ↑ +
69	+ U ↓ ↓ +
67	+ U ↓ ↓ I +
65	+ U ↓ ↓ I I +
63	+ U ↓ ↓ U I I +
61	+ U ↓ ↓ I I I I +
59	+ U ↓ ↓ I U ↓ I I +
57	+ U ↓ ↓ I U ↓ I I I +
55	+ U ↓ ↓ I U ↓ I I I I +
53	+ U ↓ ↓ I U ↓ I U ↓ I I +
51	+ U ↓ ↓ I U ↓ I U ↓ I I I +
49	+ U ↓ ↓ I U ↓ I U ↓ I I I I +
47	+ U ↓ ↓ I U ↓ I U ↓ I U ↓ I I +
45	+ U ↓ ↓ I U ↓ I U ↓ I U ↓ I I I +
43	+ U ↓ ↓ I U ↓ I U ↓ I U ↓ I I I I +
41	+ U ↓ ↓ I U ↓ I U ↓ I U ↓ I U ↓ I I +
39	+ U ↓ ↓ I U ↓ I U ↓ I U ↓ I U ↓ I I I +
37	+ U I U ↓ I U ↓ I U ↓ I U ↓ I U ↓ I I I +
35	+ U I U ↓ I U ↓ I U ↓ I U ↓ I U ↓ I I I +
33	+ U I U ↓ I U ↓ I U ↓ I U ↓ I U ↓ I I I +
31	+ U I U ↓ I U ↓ I U ↓ I U ↓ I I I +
29	+ U I U ↓ I U ↓ I U ↓ I U ↓ I I +
27	+ U I U ↓ I U ↓ I U ↓ I I I +
25	+ U I U ↓ I U ↓ I U ↓ I I +
23	+ U I U ↓ I U ↓ I I I +
21	+ U I U ↓ I U ↓ I I +
19	+ U I U ↓ I U ↓ I I I +
17	+ U I U ↓ I U ↓ I +
15	+ U I U ↓ I I +
13	+ U I U ↓ I +
11	+ U I U ↓ I +
9	+ U I U ↓ I +
7	+ U I I I +
5	+ U I I +
3	+ U I +
1	+ I +

MS = pattern

Symbols

- ✚ = 1 edge stitch
- U = 1 yarn around hook
- I = 1 plain/knit stitch
- ↓ = decrease 2 stitches together
- ↑ = decrease 3 stitches together
- MS = pattern

Stylish bag

A bag for all seasons

Size: 38 x 28cm (15 x 11in) • Level of difficulty: ✱✱✱

Materials
- Mohair acrylic wool blend – yardage approximately 70m (229ft 8in)/100g (3½oz): 300g (10½oz) in green marl
- Knooking hook 10/J (6mm)
- Bag handles, 24 x 12cm (9½ x 4¾in)

Garter stitch: plain (or knit) stitch in both directions
Tension garter stitch: 8.5 stitches and 14 rows = 10 x 10cm (4 x 4in)

Side pieces (make 2)
Starting on one side, chain 20 stitches. Transfer to the knooking hook and knook two rows in garter stitch. The right edge is the bottom of the bag and the left edge is the top. In the following row (right side) work one row as follows for the decorative drawstring section on the side: edge stitch, * knit 2, 1 yarn around hook, repeat from * 5 times, finishing with 6 purl, edge stitch.
Work these 26 stitches in garter stitch.
After two more rows, proceed as follows for the top drawstring: decrease the 19th and 20th stitches together, winding the yarn once around the hook. Repeat this 13 times in every 4th row. Then work two more rows of garter stitch over all the stitches and work one row (right side) as follows for the decorative drawstring section on the side: edge stitch, * decrease 3 stitches together, 1 yarn around hook, repeat from * five more times, finishing with 6 knit (plain) stitches and 1 edge stitch.
Knook another two rows in garter stitch over the 20 remaining stitches, then cast off.

Side/bottom strip
Chain 10 stitches, then transfer to the knooking hook and work 116 rows in garter stitch. Crochet off.

Finishing off
Place the strip under one side piece and join with slip stitches, starting and finishing under the cord drawstring. Then attach the second side piece in the same way.

Decorative drawstring (make 4)
Chain 3 stitches and work 1 double (UK treble) into the second chain, * 2 chain, then work 1 double (UK treble) into the double (UK treble), repeat four times from * and finish. Thread one decorative drawstring from top to bottom through the six holes in the sides, and sew the ends securely to the bag. Repeat with the top drawstring, but finishing after 100cm (39½in). Sew the bag handles to the inside of the bag above the cord drawstring. Thread the cord around the bag and tie in the middle of the front.

Men's scarf

Size: 14 x 180cm (5½ x 71in) • Level of difficulty: ✱

Materials
- Pure new wool – yardage approximately 70m (229ft 8in)/50g (1¾oz): 100g (3½oz) each in natural, light brown and dark brown
- Knooking hook 6/G (4mm)

Garter stitch: plain (or knit) stitches in both directions

Stripe sequence: 30 rows alternating between natural, light brown and dark brown

Tension: 14 stitches and 20 rows = 10 x 10cm (4 x 4in)

How to do it
Chain 3 stitches in natural wool. Transfer to the knooking hook and knook garter stitch in the sequence of stripes shown. To shape the scarf, from the second row from casting on, increase 1 stitch on every second row 14 times = 31 stitches.

Then to shape the scarf, on every second row twist increase 1 stitch on the right edge after the edge stitch, and on the left edge decrease the 2 stitches before the edge stitch together. After 12 stripes from casting on (the corner in the natural colour is also counted as a stripe), for the final corner decrease the 2 stitches before and after the edge stitch in every second row together, 14 times.

Cast off the last 3 stitches.

One for the boys

20

Children's striped beanie

Size: 46–50cm (18–19¾in) • Level of difficulty: ✶✶

Materials

- Wool acrylic blend – yardage approximately 120m (393ft 8½in)/100g (3½oz): 100g (3½oz) green-brown colour
- Knooking hook 6/G (4mm)

Stocking stitch in rounds: all stocking stitch
Tension: 14 stitches and 21 rows = 10 x 10cm (4 x 4in)

How to do it

Chain 64 stitches and join with a slip stitch to make a circle. Transfer to the knooking hook. Work in stocking stitch. After 24 rounds from casting on, decrease every seventh and eighth stitch together in the following round = 56 stitches. In the following third round, decrease every sixth and seventh stitch together = 48 stitches. Repeat these decreases in the same places five more times in every second round.

Draw the working thread through the 8 remaining stitches and secure.

Nature lovers

Brown beanie

Size: 54–58cm (21¼–22¾in) • Level of difficulty: ✹✹

Materials

- Cotton acrylic blend – yardage approximately 65m (213ft 3in)/50g (1¾oz): 100g (3½oz) brown
- Knooking hook 6/G (4mm)

Rib pattern worked in rounds: knit 1, purl 1 in turn
Stocking stitch in rounds: all stocking stitch
Stripe sequence: knit six rounds stocking stitch and one round purl, in turn
Tension: 13 stitches and 17 rows = 10 x 10cm (4 x 4in)

How to do it

Chain 72 stitches and join with a slip stitch to make a circle. Transfer to the knooking hook. For the rim, work six rounds in a rib pattern, and continue in the sequence of the stripes. After 30 rounds = 16.5cm (6½in) from the rim, in the following round decrease every seventh and eighth stitch together = 63 stitches. In the following third round, decrease every sixth and seventh stitch together = 54 stitches. Repeat these decreases in the same places twice in every third round, and twice in every second round. Draw the working thread through the 18 remaining stitches and secure.

Green beanie

Size: 52–56cm (20½–22in) • Level of difficulty: ★★★

Materials

- Wool acrylic blend – yardage approximately 100m (328ft)/50g (1¾oz): 100g (3½oz) green
- Knooking hook 6/G (4mm)

Rib pattern worked in rounds: knit 1, purl 1 in turn
Stocking stitch in rounds: all stocking stitch
Tension: 15 stitches and 21 rows = 10 x 10cm (4 x 4in)

How to do it

Chain 80 stitches and join with a slip stitch to make a circle. Transfer to the knooking hook. Work six rounds in rib pattern for the rim, then knook in stocking stitch. Increase 1 stitch in every fourth stitch in the first round = 100 stitches. After 24 rounds from casting on, in the following round decrease every 24th and 25th stitch together = 96 stitches. Repeat these decreases in the same places twice more in every fourth round = 88 stitches. In the following second round, decrease every seventh and eighth stitch together = 77 stitches. Repeat these decreases in the same places six more times in every second round. Draw the working thread through the 11 remaining stitches and secure.

Is he looking at me …

… or my cool hat?

Wrist warmers

Size: one size fits all • Level of difficulty: ✳ ✳

Material

- Wool acrylic blend – yardage approximately 55m (180ft 5½in)/50g (1¾oz): 100g (3½oz) orange and 50g (1¾oz) petrol
- Knooking hook 6/G (4mm)

Rib pattern worked in rounds: knit 2, purl 2 in turn
Stocking stitch in rounds: all stocking stitch
Stripe sequence: three rounds in petrol and six rounds in orange in turn
Tension: 12 stitches and 17 rows = 10 x 10cm (4 x 4in)

How to do it

Starting on the front edge, chain 24 stitches in orange and join with a slip stitch to make a circle. Transfer to the knooking hook. Knook in rib stitch.

To make the thumbhole, eight rounds after casting on cast on 8 chain between 2 purl stitches and include in the rib pattern in the next round. For the thumb section of the glove, in every second round twist decrease the stitch before the first thumb stitch with it (purl), and decrease the last thumb stitch with the following stitch (purl) = two decreases in each round. Repeat these decreases in the same places three more times in every second round = 24 stitches. Then work 18 more rounds in the stripe sequence. Cast off loosely.

Fingerless gloves and ...

... cuddly and warm

26

Baby shoes

Brightly coloured birds

Tablet and phone cover

Hot water bottle cover

Checked pillowcase

Indoors

Whether it's a doorstop, a pillowcase or a cuddly blanket for a little one – you'll be amazed at what you can make.

Baby's hat

Doorstop

Chair leg covers

Patchwork blanket

Doorstop

Size: 25cm (9¾in) high • Level of difficulty: ✱✱

I'll keep watch!

Materials
- Tweed acrylic wool blend – yardage approximately 100m (328ft) /100g (3½oz): 200g (7oz) green
- Knooking hook 6/G (4mm)
- 2 round buttons for the eyes
- 1 triangular button for the nose
- Scraps of grey cotton yarn for the whiskers
- Toy stuffing
- Pebbles or gravel

Stocking stitch in rounds: all stocking stitch
Tension: 14 stitches and 18 rows = 10 x 10cm (4 x 4in)

Body
Starting with the head, chain 48 stitches and join with a slip stitch to make a circle. Transfer to the knooking hook. Knook in stocking stitch. After 20 rounds from casting on, from the next round increase 1 stitch in every eighth stitch six times = 54 stitches. After four more rounds, increase 6 stitches evenly = 60 stitches. Then knook 24 rounds in stocking stitch. For the base, decrease every 14th and 15th stitch in the next round together = 56 stitches. In the following second round, decrease every sixth and seventh stitch together = 48 stitches. In the following second round, decrease every fifth and sixth stitch together = 40 stitches. Repeat these decreases in the same places four more times in every second round. Draw the working yarn through the 8 remaining stitches and secure.

Tail
Chain 12 stitches and join with a slip stitch to make a circle. Transfer to the knooking hook. Knook in stocking stitch.
After 30cm (11¾in) from casting on, in the following round decrease every third and fourth stitch together = 9 stitches. In the following second round, decrease every second and third stitch together. Draw the working yarn through the 6 remaining stitches and secure.

Finishing off
Fill the base of the body with some pebbles or gravel to give it weight and fill the rest with the toy stuffing. Place the casting on edge flat together and sew up the seam, slightly gathering the middle four stitches.
Fill the tail with more toy stuffing. Sew up the casting on edge, and sew the tail to the back of the body. Sew on the buttons for the eyes and nose. Sew on the whiskers as illustrated.

Baby's hat

Size: for 3–12 months • Level of difficulty: ✱

Materials

- Cotton yarn – yardage approximately 90m
  (295ft 3½in)/50g (1¾oz): 50g (1¾oz) pastel colour
- Knooking hook 6/G (4mm)

Garter stitch: plain (or knit) stitches in
both directions
Tension: 16 stitches and 30 rows = 10 x 10cm
(4 x 4in)

How to do it

Chain 27 stitches and transfer them onto the knooking
hook. Knit in garter stitch.
To make the right ear flap, after eight rows from casting on
increase 1 stitch on the right edge four times in every second row, then work eight rows of 31 stitches. Decrease 1
stitch on the right edge four times in every second row.
Work 20 rows with 27 stitches, then make the left ear flap
in the same way.
Work another eight rows with 27 stitches, then cast off.

Finishing off

Sew up the hat seam using kitchener stitch and tighten
the straight edge. Take up every second edge stitch with
yarn and pull tight.
Work one round of slip stitches into the stitches along
the front of the hat. To make the ties, chain 30 stitches
and join to the ear flap with 1 slip stitch. Slip stitch back
along the chain stitches to the beginning.
Knot the threads at the beginning and
end together.

Here's lookin at you kid ...

Brightly coloured birds

Size: any · Level of difficulty: ✱

Materials

- Wool acrylic blend – yardage approximately 100m (328ft)/50g (1¾oz): yarn remnants in any colours
- Knooking hook 6/G (4mm)
- Toy stuffing
- 2 small buttons for each bird

Garter stitch in rounds: 1 round knit, 1 round purl in turn
Tension: 16 stitches and 32 rows = 10 x 10cm (4 x 4in)

How to do it

Work the birds in squares. For a bird measuring 10 x 10cm (4 x 4in): chain 32 stitches and join with a slip stitch to make a circle. Knook 10cm (4in) in garter stitch, then cast off.

Finishing off

Place the casting on edge flat together and sew up. Place the finishing edge together and sew up, fill the inside with toy stuffing when you are about halfway. For the feet, chain 5 stitches + 1 turning chain and work in single crochet (UK double).
* In the next row, single crochet (UK double) the first 2 stitches, then work 3 chain + 1 turning chain and single crochet (UK double) back on these 3 chain + 2 single crochet (UK double). Repeat once from *, then finish. Sew the feet to the casting on edge.
To make the beak, chain 8 stitches and turn with 1 additional chain, then crochet the 8 chain as follows: 1 slip stitch, 1 single crochet (UK double), 1 half double (UK half treble), 2 double (UK treble), 1 half double (UK half treble), 1 single crochet (UK double crochet), 1 slip stitch, finish. Fold the beak in half along the middle and sew the edge to the bird.
Sew buttons on both sides of the head as the eyes.

Pretty playmates

Hot water bottle cover

Size: 19 x 32cm (7½ x 12½in) · Level of difficulty: ✱

For a cold night ...

Materials

- Cotton acrylic blend – yardage approximately 65m (213ft 3in)/50g (1¾oz): 50g (1¾oz) each in turquoise, coral and mint
- Knooking hook 6/G (4mm)
- Hot water bottle, 18 x 30cm (7 x 11¾in)

Garter stitch: plain (or knit) stitch in both directions
Stripe sequence, garter stitch: rows 1 to 14: 10 stitches in mint, 9 stitches in coral, 10 stitches in turquoise; rows 15 and 16: all stitches in mint; rows 17 and 18: 10 stitches in mint, 9 stitches in coral, 10 stitches in turquoise; rows 19 to 26: repeat rows 15 to 18 twice; rows 27 and 28: all stitches in mint; rows 29 to 56: repeat rows 1 to 28 once; rows 57 to 80: repeat rows 1 to 14 once.
Ribbing: knit 1, purl 1 in turn
Tension garter stitch: 15 stitches and 28 rows = 10 x 10cm (4 x 4in)

Front

Starting at the bottom edge, chain 10 stitches in turquoise, 9 in coral and 10 in mint. Transfer onto the knooking hook and work in garter stitch in the sequence of the stripes. After 80 rows from casting on, work the drawstring as follows in turquoise: edge stitch, * decrease 2 stitches together, yarn around, and repeat from *, finishing with 1 knit (plain) and the edge stitch.
In the following row (wrong side), knook all stitches in stocking stitch, then work eight rows in rib for the neck and cast off.

Back

Work in the same way.

Drawstring (make 2)

Work chain stitches to a length of approximately 50cm (19¾in) in coral, then slip stitch into each chain.

Finishing off

Place front and back together with the wrong sides facing, and backstitch up the sides and along the bottom edge in turquoise. Insert the hook after the edge stitch on the side seams, and above the casting on row along the bottom. Thread one cord through the front and the second one through the back, from right to left, below the neck and knot at the sides.

Baby shoes

Size: UK 1–2, for 3–6 months (US 2 –3) (European 62–68) • Level of difficulty: ✱

Materials

- Wool acrylic blend – yardage approximately 55m (180ft 5½in)/50g (1¾oz): 50g (1¾oz) in vanilla
- Knooking hook 6/G (4mm)
- 2 stitch markers
- Ribbon or cord

Garter stitch: plain (or knit) stitches in both directions
Tension: 12 stitches and 20 rows = 10 x 10cm (4 x 4in)

How to do it

Chain 32 stitches and transfer onto the knooking hook. Knit in garter stitch.

After ten rows from casting on, mark the tenth stitch in and the tenth stitch from the end. In the following row, decrease the first marked stitch with the following stitch, and the second marked stitch with the stitch in front of it = 30 stitches.

Repeat these decreases in every second row three more times. Cast off the remaining 24 stitches for the sole.

Finishing off

Place the sole stitches together and sew up the seams. There should be 9 ribs to each side of the sole seam. The 3 ribs to the right and left of the sole seam are the sole. Place the 6 ribs on the right over the sole, and the 6 ribs on the left over the sole as a third layer, and sew up this triple seam from inside. Turn the shoe right side out. Thread the ribbon through to the left and right of the flap and tie.

Note

Fold the soles of the right and left over in the opposite ways, as mirror images of each other.

Baby steps

Patchwork blanket

Sizes: 80 x 80cm (31½ x 31½in) • Level of difficulty: ✱✱

Materials

- Pure new wool – yardage approximately 90m (295ft 3½in)/50g (1¾oz): 150g (5¼oz) each in natural, brown and light blue
- Knooking hook 6/G (4mm)

Garter stitch: plain (or knit) stitches in both directions

Stocking stitch: right side knit, wrong side purl Purl: right side purl, wrong side knit

Ribbing: knit 1, purl 1 in turn

Seed stitch: knit 1, purl 1 continuously, but reversing the sequence after every row

Check pattern (over 12 stitches): rows 1 to 4: purl 4 stitches, knit 4 stitches, purl 4 stitches;

rows 5 to 8: knit 4 stitches, purl 4 stitches, knit 4 stitches;

rows 9 to 12: as rows 1-4.

Patch: chain 22 stitches and work as follows between the edge stitches: Patch 1: rows 1 to 8: garter stitch; rows 9 to 24 as follows: 4 garter stitches, 12 seed stitches, 4 garter stitches. rows 25 to 32: garter stitch.

Patch 2: as Patch 1, working rows 9 to 24 as follows: 4 garter stitches, 12 seed stitches, 4 garter stitches. Patch 3: as Patch 1, working rows 9 to 24 as follows: 4 garter stitches, 12 stitches check pattern, 12 garter stitches.

Tension: 1 Patch = 13 x 13cm (5 x 5in)

How to do it

Knook 36 patches as per the diagram and sew together on the wrong side, catching the edge stitches in the seam. The arrows in the diagram indicate the direction of work; be sure to follow them.

Diagram

B3	→ N1	L2	→ B3	N1	→ L2
→ N2	L3	→ B1	N2	→ L3	B1
L1	→ B2	N3	→ L1	B2	→ N3
→ B3	N1	→ L2	B3	→ N1	L2
N2	→ L3	B1	→ N2	L3	→ B1
→ L1	B2	→ N3	L1	→ B2	N3

Symbols

1 = Patch 1   N = Natural
2 = Patch 2   B = Brown
3 = Patch 3   L = Light blue

Finishing off

Work one row of single crochet (UK double) around the blanket in brown and light blue, working 3 single crochet (UK double) in the same stitch in the corners. Finish with one round of picots in natural (= * 1 single crochet/UK double), 3 chain and 1 single crochet/UK double) back into the first chain, miss 1 stitch, repeat from *).

Checked pillowcase

Size: 40 x 40cm (15¾ x 15¾in) • Level of difficulty: ✳

Materials
- Wool acrylic blend – yardage approximately 55m (180ft 5½in)/50g (1¾oz): 300g (10½oz) in natural
- Knooking hook 10/J (6mm)
- Cushion 40 x 40cm (15¾ x 15¾in)

Garter stitch: plain (or knit) stitches in both directions
Ribbing: knit 1, purl 1 in turn
Tension: 11 stitches and 18 rows = 10 x 10cm (4 x 4in)

How to do it

Chain 47 stitches and transfer them onto the knooking hook. Between the edge stitches, work 9 garter stitches and 9 rib stitches alternately, finishing with 9 garter stitches. Change the pattern after 18 rows from casting on. After 36 rows from casting on, repeat the pattern three more times.
This should give a total of 144 rows = 80cm (31½in) from casting on. Cast off.

Finishing off
Fold in half and sew up the side seams.
Put the cushion inside and sew up the top and bottom seams.

Cuddle up or ...

... have a pillow fight!

Tablet and phone covers

Size: tablet cover 19 x 24cm (7½ x 9½in); phone cover 7 x 13cm (2¾ x 5in) • Level of difficulty: ✷✷

Materials
- Cotton acrylic blend – yardage approximately 65m (213ft 3in)/50g (1¾oz): 50g (1¾oz) each in black and white
- Knooking hook 6/G (4mm)

Stocking stitch in rounds: all stocking stitch
Weave pattern A in rounds: even number of stitches: rounds one and two in black: stocking stitch; round three in white: * lift off 1 stitch, keeping the yarn behind your work, knit 1, repeat from *; rounds four and five in white: stocking stitch; round six in black: work as round three. Repeat rounds one to six throughout.
Weave pattern B: work as weave pattern A, but swap the colours.
Ribbing: knit 1, purl 1 in turn
Weave pattern tension: 15.5 stitches and 25 rows = 10 x 10cm (4 x 4in)

How to make the tablet cover
Chain 60 stitches in black and join with a slip stitch to make a circle. Transfer the stitches onto the knooking hook. Work in stocking stitch. After 10 rounds from casting on, work the next 36 rounds in weave pattern A, then knook five rounds in stocking stitch in black. For the cuff, work three rounds in rib, then cast off.

Finishing off
Fold in half with the sides of the casting on edge together, and sew up using kitchener stitch.

How to make the phone cover
Chain 24 stitches in white and join with a slip stitch to make a circle. Transfer the stitches onto the knooking hook. Work in stocking stitch. After four rounds from casting on, work the next 18 rounds in weave pattern B, then knook three more rounds in stocking stitch in white. For the cuff, work rounds in rib, then cast off.

Finishing off
See instructions for tablet cover.

Trendy and chic

Chair leg covers

Size: 14 x 7cm (5½ x 2¾in) wide • Level of difficulty: ✸ ✸

Materials

- Alpaca polyester wool blend – yardage approximately 120m (393ft 8½in)/50g (1¾oz)): 50g (1¾oz) each in blue/red and grey
- Knooking hook 10/J (6mm)

Rib pattern worked in rounds: knit 2, purl 2 in turn
Stripe sequence: 5 rounds blue/red, 2 rounds grey, 4 rounds blue/red, 2 rounds grey, 4 rounds blue/red, 2 rounds grey, 5 rounds blue/red
Tension: 17 stitches and 17 rows = 10 x 10cm (4 x 4in) (very slightly stretched).

How to do it

Starting at the bottom edge, chain 24 stitches in blue/red and join with a slip stitch to make a circle. Transfer the stitches onto the knooking hook. Work in rib stitches, following the sequence of the stripes. Cast off loosely after 24 rounds from the beginning or when the cover is as long as you want it.

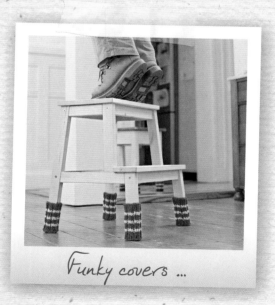

Funky covers ...

... for wooden legs

Publication details

First published in Great Britain in 2015 by
Search Press Limited
Wellwood, North Farm Road,
Tunbridge Wells, Kent TN2 3DR

Original edition © 2014
World rights reserved by Christophorus Verlag GmbH,
Freiburg/Germany
Original German title:
Knooking Stricken mit der Häkelnadel

English translation by Burravoe Translation Services

Design and text: Veronika Hug
Projects by: Veronika Hug and Christel Hurst
Photography: Florian Bilger Fotodesign
Styling: Peggy Kummerow
Knitting charts and patterns: Carsten Bachmann
and Sabine Schidelko

ISBN 978-1-78221-224-9

Suppliers

If you have difficulty in obtaining any of the materials and
equipment mentioned in this book, then please visit the Search
Press website for details of suppliers: www.searchpress.com

Printed in China